PHP

Basic Fundamental Guide for Beginners

TABLE OF CONTENTS

Introduction to PHP

Is this your first time to code in PHP? Are you stuck in the MySQL database? Perhaps you don't know how to create sessions or cookies in PHP? This book will take you through a complete step-by-step process of learning PHP. Whether you have just started or you want to continue from where you left, get this masterpiece containing the fundamental concepts of PHP.

Besides that, we will explain everything in a friendly and interactive manner to make sure that you understand every concept. We will also provide you with screenshots of source code to type in your favorite text editor.

If your goal is to become a great PHP developer, then this book is for you. If you want to quickly master the basic fundamentals of PHP programming, then this book will help you do so. If you are tired of debugging your code and you want to learn how you can fix it up fast, then we have the solution for you.

PHP is an amazing language with easy-to-understand concepts. If you can learn PHP today, then you will manage to create anything from a simple contact form to a complete web application. You will even learn how to create a mailing list or a content management system.

That said, this book will teach you how to do that. We will also teach you how to build PHP applications to solve real-world problems. Since PHP is a web-based language, a little knowledge of HTML and CSS will help you. Still, if you're green on HTML and CSS. Don't worry, HTML and CSS are just easy as 1, 2, and 3.

Chapter 1

Starting Up and Running With PHP

Introduction to PHP

Welcome to PHP. A popular programming language used by many people across the world.

PHP is an amazing language which you can use to build interactive and dynamic websites. When you are done writing your PHP program, you must have a Web server to run your code. PHP programs serve web pages to visitors based on their request. Put simply, it is a server side language. PHP has one prominent feature where you can embed your written code within the pages of HTML. This makes it very easy for anyone who wants to make dynamic content.

In the previous paragraph, you can simply say I described PHP as 'interactive and dynamic.'

As a beginner to PHP programming, you may be wondering about what exactly those two phrases mean. To save you time, when you hear a programmer describe a web page as being dynamic, they are simply trying to say that the contents of the page change automatically whenever the page is viewed. You can compare this with a static HTML file which never changes no matter how many people visit the page. Meanwhile, an interactive web page is one which accepts and responds to the input it receives from the visitors. A good example of an interactive website is a web forum. In a web forum, different users can post a message which is then displayed on the forum for everyone to see.

If you have been wondering what PHP stands for, then you are in the right place. PHP is an abbreviation for Hypertext Preprocessor. By just knowing the full meaning of PHP, you can begin to tell some of the capabilities of the language. In simple terms, it processes information and unveils it as hypertext. Many developers prefer recursive acronyms and PHP is very appealing to developers.

In PHP, for you to see the results after you have written your code, you must run your program on a PHP server. Below are the steps to follow if you want to run your PHP program on a Web server:

1. First, a visitor will make a request for a web page by either typing the URL of the webpage or clicking on a link. The visitor can send data to the web server as well with the help of a form attached to the web page.

2. The server finds out which type of request it is, once it knows that the language is PHP. It begins processing the request.

3. Once the processing is completed, the visitor sees a page.

The most exciting thing takes place when the PHP program runs. Since PHP is a very flexible language, a single PHP script can perform a multitude of interesting tasks. Some of the tasks it can perform are:

- Process details in a form

- Read and write files on a web server

- It can process data kept in a web server which has a database

- Build dynamic graphics

Lastly, when any of the above tasks are done, a PHP script can show a customized HTML web page to the visitor.

Why should I use PHP?

Most people new to PHP always ask this question. If you happen to be among them, here is something interesting for you, many internet service providers and web hosting firms have systems that are compatible with PHP. Today, a big population of developers use PHP, and they are very many because a majority of the websites are built on PHP programming.

Another powerful feature that you will get, if you choose to use the PHP language, is that it's cross-platform compatible. What this one simply means is that you can run your PHP programs on more than one platform. It doesn't matter if the platform you're using is Mac OS X, Windows, FreeBSD, and Solaris. Plus, the PHP engine is compatible with some of the popular web servers like Internet Information Server, Zeus, Apache, and lighttpd. This implies that if you want to develop your PHP program in, let's say, a Windows setup and later deploy it on Mac OS X, it is possible. In addition, the process of migrating your entire PHP program is easy. No stress involved.

Now, before we begin to discuss the basics of PHP language. I want to briefly show you the steps in setting up your PHP environment. Then, you can learn how to write a simple PHP code.

First PHP Code

What you should have

For you to actually run your first PHP script, you have to install and run a PHP Web server. You can pick any of the choices below:

- **Run localhost on your computer**

In this option, you will be running PHP on your computer. In other words, you will install a local PHP Web server on your machine. The easiest way you can achieve this is by looking online for a complete package. XAMPP is one of the best choices you should go for. This comes with the Apache Web server, MySQL database engine, PHP, and many other applications. No stress when it comes to the installation. Just a click of a button and you'll be done.

- **Run your coded scripts on a web host**

Now, if you have an active web hosting account which is designed to allow PHP, you can run your PHP scripts there. What you will do is use the FTP to upload your scripts. If you upload everything, then you can run the server to see the results. The disadvantage with a web server is that it is not fast compared to a local host.

Your First Script

Below is a script of PHP that you will learn how to create.

```
<Code />

<!DOCTYPE html PUBLIC "-//W3C//DTD XHTML 1.0 Strict//EN"
  "http://www.w3.org/TR/xhtml1/DTD/xhtml1-strict.dtd">
<html xmlns="http://www.w3.org/1999/xhtml" xml:lang="en" lang="en">
  <head>
    <title>My first PHP script</title>
  </head>
  <body>
    <p><?php echo "Hello, world!"; ?></p>
  </body>
</html>
```

In the above script, the majority is made up of XHTML.

So, the <? Php and ?> tags pass a message to the Web server that everything in the tags is a PHP code. The line of code enclosed within the PHP tags is simple. It makes use of a built-in function called 'echo,' which prints a simple text ("Hello, world!") on the website. The PHP language has a lot of functions which we are going to learn in the following chapters. These functions are important to help a developer or programmer build applications.

You should pay attention to the semicolon (;) immediately after the line of PHP. The semicolon shows the end of the PHP line of code. Every time you finish writing your line of PHP, you should put a semicolon. However, if you are writing a single line of code like in the example above, then it is optional. You can choose to put it in or ignore it. But, not when you have more than one line of PHP script.

Creating the PHP script

Now, for you to create a similar script like the one above, first, you must get a text editor. Nowadays, many computers have their own text editors such as:

6

- Windows notepad and the text editor for the MAC

However, if you feel like the above options are not the best for you, then you can choose to download Sublime text. Once you have your text editor ready, you should type the code below in the editor. Save it in any name but make sure you store in the pathway of your web server:

```
<html>
<head>
 <title>PHP Test</title>
</head>
<body>
<?php echo '<p>Hello World</p>'; ?>
</body>
</html>
```

However, if you have a web hosting account, use FTP to upload your code before you run it.

Test the script

We will now assume that you have done everything outlined above. The only thing remaining is to run your script. If you want to run your script, enter the following URLs into your web address:

- http://localhost/hello.php

For those who are working on an internet hosting account. Your code will resemble:

- http://www.youurl.com/hello.php

If everything runs well, then this is the output which you should get:

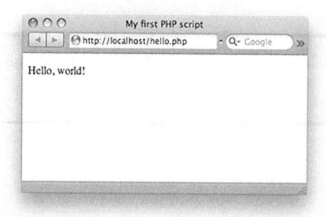

Problems?

If you encountered problems along the way while running your PHP script, you may need to go back and assess your Web server. It could be that your Web server isn't set up correctly. If for example, if the PHP code was shown on the browser instead of something similar to the above image, then that means your web server was configured well.

Next?

If the above web page displayed, congratulations! You can now write, save, and run your PHP program. You will improve the skills mentioned above in the next chapters. But for now, we are going to teach you the core basics of the PHP programming language.

Chapter 2

A Walk Through the PHP Language

At this point, you have now learned what PHP is and what some of its uses are. I believe you that you were able to run your first PHP program. Now, in this chapter, we are going to help you learn more about the core basics of PHP. This chapter will focus on:

- Variables

- PHP operators

- Constants

- Data types and many others

Variables in PHP

One of the most important things in any programming language is variables. A variable can be described as a container which can carry certain values. With variables, some values can change in the process of execution. And it's this ability to manage dynamic values which makes the variables so powerful in programming.

For instance, let's look at this line of PHP code:

echo 4 + 4;

As you might predict, this script will print 8 when it's executed. This is beautiful, but let's say, you want to show the value of 3+ 4. The only way out is to write the code like the one shown below:

echo 3 + 4;

Now, this is when variables become useful. If you decide to use variables rather than numbers in your code, then your script becomes more flexible and useful. Here is an example to show you how variables can be used:

Echo $a + $b;

The line of code above is general. But, it gives you much flexibility because you can assign any numbers to variables $a and $b. In its current state, if you were to execute this code, it will show you the sum of the values of $a and $b.

$a=4;

$b=3;

Echo $a + $b;

Naming variables

A variable is made of two parts. Those two parts consist of the variable name together with the value the variable carries. A good practice when it comes to naming your variables is to use names which are familiar to the task or operation performed. Similar to other programming languages, there are rules one must follow when giving names to variables:

- Variable names should have the dollar sign at the start

- After the dollar sign, a letter or underscore is permitted

Another important point which you need to remember is PHP variable names are case-sensitive. This means if you write *$Variable* and later write *$variable*, they are all different. I will suggest you pick one method which you will use to write all your variables and stick to that method. If you can do this, then you will avoid confusion. Again, while the length of a variable is not fixed, it is good to note that having a variable name with more than 30 characters looks abnormal. If you want to see what variables look like in PHP, then here is an example:

- *$_342*

- *$my_variable*

- *$y*

- *$number*

Declaring a variable

Declaring a PHP variable is what many developers call 'creating a variable.' To declare a variable is not something hard to do because it's very easy. For example:

$my_second_variable;

If PHP recognizes a variable's name in the code, it immediately declares the variable.

Any time you declare a variable in PHP, it's recommended that you assign the variable a value. This procedure of allocating a value to your variable is called 'initializing.' Doing this has many advantages. For example, if someone else passes through your code, they would be able to tell what type of value the variable holds. If you fail to initialize a variable, then the default value assigned is null. Have a look at how you can declare and initialize a PHP variable by trying this example:

$money=200;

Types of PHP data

All data types kept in PHP variables come in either one of the eight basic types. In the PHP language, there are four scalar data types. Data

11

is said to be scalar if it contains just a single value. Below is a list of these data types:

- **Integer**

- **Float**

It is a floating point number like 9.34

- **String**

Consists of a series of characters such as 'How much?'

- **Boolean**

This can either be false or true

Besides the scalar types, PHP also has what we call 'compound data' types. A data type is said to be compound if it can have more than one value. Listed below are the compound data types found in PHP:

- **Array**

Represents an ordered map that has numbers or names linked to values

- **Object**

One that may have methods and properties

Lastly, PHP also has special data types. They are special since they neither contain compound or scalar data. However, they have a unique meaning:

- **Resource**

- **Null**

It might have null as the value. This means the variable does not hold any value

PHP loose typing

Something else that you need to understand about PHP is it is a loosely-typed language. In other words, it is a language which does not care about the type of data kept in a variable. What this means is that it automatically changes the variable's data type. For example, you can initialize a variable as a double integer, but add a string value to it. This is not something you can do with other programming languages like Java, which is strongly-typed.

This feature of PHP is both negative and positive. It gives you the flexibility important in different situations, but on the other hand, you will not be notified if you happen to pass a wrong data type. You will not be notified of an error, but you may notice that the output of your code is not what you expected. The good news is that PHP has a way to test this.

Expressions and Operators

Now, I believe you that you are already knowledgeable about the PHP variables, right? If somebody asks you to declare and initialize an integer variable, you are capable of doing it, right? But, programming could look dull if this is only what you could achieve with variables. This is when operators bring in a new flavor. Operators allow you to play around with the data stored in the variables so that you can come up with a new value. Take, for example, the code below. It uses the operator (-) to subtract the values of $a and $b to produce a new value:

- *echo $a-$b;*

In short, if you are still wondering what an operator is, it is a symbol with the ability to change one or more values, often resulting in a new value. On the other hand, an expression is anything which will translate into a value. This can consist of different combinations of functions, operators, variables, and values. In the previous example, $a-$b is an expression. Some other examples of expressions are:

- *$x - $y*

- *True*

- *$x + $y + $t*

Operands are the values and variables used together with an operator.

Types of operators

There are 10 types of operators in PHP. They are:

- **Arithmetic operators**

These include addition, subtraction, multiplication, division, and modulus

- **Assignment operators (=)**

You have already seen its application

- **Bitwise operators**

- **Comparison operators**

This lets you make comparisons between one operand and the other one in different ways.

Here's a list of the comparison operators in PHP:

Operator	Example	Result
== (equal)	$x == $y	true if $x equals $y; false otherwise
!= or <> (not equal)	$x != $y	true if $x does not equal $y; false otherwise
=== (identical)	$x === $y	true if $x equals $y and they are of the same type; false otherwise
!== (not identical)	$x !== $y	true if $x does not equal $y or they are not of the same type; false otherwise
< (less than)	$x < $y	true if $x is less than $y; false otherwise
> (greater than)	$x > $y	true if $x is greater than $y; false otherwise
<= (less than or equal to)	$x <= $y	true if $x is less than or equal to $y; false otherwise
>= (greater than or equal to)	$x >= $y	true if $x is greater than or equal to $y; false otherwise

- **Incrementing and decrementing operators**

Usually used to subtract or add the value one over and over again

- **Logical operators**

These work on the Boolean values. A Boolean value can either be true or false

- **String operators**

PHP has only one string operator which is the concatenation operator or the (dot). What this string operator does is to join two strings to make them longer.

Operator precedence

When dealing with a simple expression such as 4 + 9, it is very easy. Add 4 and 9 to get 13. But, let's examine a case where we have more than one operator, do you think we shall work it out the same way we did above? No! This is when operator precedence comes in to help. All operators in PHP have been ordered based on precedence. This means

15

that an operator with higher precedence is always executed first before one which has a lower precedence. Below is a list of operators arranged according to precedence.

Precedence of Some PHP Operators (Highest First)
++ -- (increment/decrement)
(int) (float) (string) (array) (object) (bool) (casting)
! (not)
* / % (arithmetic)
+ - . (arithmetic)
< <= > >= <> (comparison)
== != === !== (comparison)
&& (and)
|| (or)
= += -= *= /= .= %= (assignment)
and
xor
or

Constants

PHP also allows you to define constants to hold values. One thing about the values of constants is that it remains the same. In addition, constants are defined once in a PHP script.

Don't confuse constants with variables in PHP. Constants are different from variables in the way they are defined, and they don't begin with the dollar sign. However, I will recommend that you make it a habit to define all your constants in uppercase letters. In addition, don't use reserved PHP keywords to define constants. If you do so, you may confuse PHP.

Decisions and Loops

Up to this point, you have learned some of the basics of PHP. You know the number of data types in PHP, and you know the types of expressions in PHP as well as variables, right? All of the codes you have seen are categorized as a linear type of code. But, things become even interesting when you begin to use decisions and loops.

Simply put, a decision will allow you to either execute a given section of code or not depending on the results of a given test. Loops will permit the code to run repeatedly until that point when the code accomplishes a specific condition.

By integrating decisions and loops into your code, you will gain much control over your code, and you can make them dynamic. With the help of decisions and loops, you have a chance to display different kinds of content to your visitors depending on what buttons they click or where they live, among other conditions.

Making decisions

Similar to other popular programming languages, PHP gives you the power to write a code which can make a decision, depending on the current result of an expression. With 'decisions,' you have the ability to develop complex codes.

Decisions with 'If statements'

This is the easiest decision statement that one can understand. The basic nature of the 'if statement' is as follows:

If (expression) {

// put here your code

}

// additional code goes here

17

In this example, the code in the braces is executed only if the expression in the parenthesis is true.

Now, let's say the code is false, then that means the code in the braces will not be executed. However, it is important to highlight that any script after the closing brace will always be executed no matter the results of the test. So in the previous example, if the expression is true, then both the 'put here your code' and the 'additional code goes here' will run. But, if the expression is found to be false, then the 'put here your code' will not be executed, but the extra 'additional code goes here' will still be executed.

Another 'else statement'

You have seen that the 'if statement' will let you execute a code if an expression is true. But, if the expression is read as false, then the piece of code is skipped. Now, with an else statement, it gives you the ability to improve the decision-making process. Let's look at an example:

If ($z >=20) {

echo "Z is greater than twenty";

} else {

echo "Z is less than 20";

}

If z is greater than or equal to twenty, then 'Z is greater than twenty' is displayed. However, if Z is less than twenty, then 'Z is less than 20' is shown to the user. It is still possible to create a combination of a 'last else' statement with another 'if' statement, so you have plenty of alternative choices. PHP still offers you with a special 'else, if' in which you can combine an 'else' and 'if' statement. So you can have it like this:

```
If (expression1) {

echo "Write your statement here";

} else if (expression2) {

echo "Write your second statement here";

} else {

echo "write your last statement here";

}
```

Switch statement

There are times when you will face a scenario where you want to test an expression against many different values, each having its own assigned task if the value matches. Have a look at this example that applies to the 'if,' 'else, if' and 'else' statements:

```
If ($x === "open") {

// Open the file

} else if ($x == "save") {

// Save the file

} else if ($x == "logout") {

// logout the user

} else {

Print "Kindly select an option";

}
```

The above example repeatedly compares the same variable with different values. Well, this is very tiresome. What if you want to have a different expression?

If you were to implement it with the PHP switch statement, things just get easier and fun. The switch statement makes things look simple and elaborate. You will use the expression 'once.' You can look at the example so that you can understand what I am saying:

Switch ($X) {

case "open":

//Open your file

break;

case "save":

// save your file

break;

case "logout":

//logout the user

break;

default:

print "kindly select an option";

}

You can see that despite the second example requiring additional lines of code, it is a clear approach that is easy to follow and maintain.

Using the ternary operator

We already looked at operators in the previous sections, has and there is another operator known as the ternary operator. The ternary operator has the question mark as its symbol. Furthermore, the ternary operator evaluates three expressions:

(expression 1)? expression2: expression3;

The ternary operator is somehow similar to the 'if, else' construct. You can think of the ternary operator as a compact version of the 'if, else' style. The previous code can be interpreted like this: 'If the *expression1* is true, then the entire expression is equal to *expression1on2*, but if the *expression1* is evaluated as false, then the overall expression is equal to *expression1on3.*"

Using loops to do repeated tasks

I hope you have learned how you can make decisions with a separate snippet of code based on a written condition. Now, I want to introduce to you something more powerful. I know you have heard of the word loop. As the name suggests, there is an act of repetition in a loop. So, a loop repeats a given task until a condition is attained. Similar to decisions, the condition in a 'loop' has to be in the form of an expression. For those of you who don't understand this, let me explain it to you. If the expression is going to be false, then the loop will stop. But, as long as it is true, the loop continues to run.

While loops

This is the easiest type of loop that anyone can understand. A 'while' loop looks similar to the 'if' statement. Here is a 'while' construct:

While (expression) {

//Code

}

// More code

Looks simple, doesn't it? If the expression found in the parenthesis is evaluated and found to be true, the block of code in the braces is executed. Again, if the expression is evaluated and found to be true, then the block of code is executed again, and the pattern goes on. However, let's say the expression is false, what happens? The loop exits the condition, but the remaining code outside the parenthesis will be executed. Let us use a practical application of a 'while' loop:

```php
<? php
$books= 10;
while ($books > 0) {
echo "Selling a book... ";
$books - -;
echo "done. There are $books books left. < br / >";
}
echo "We are out of books!";
? >
```

The 'do while' loop

In the 'while loop,' we evaluate the expression at the start. However, when it comes to the 'do while' we do the opposite. We first run part of the code before we test the expression. Look at this example:

```php
<? php
$w = 1;
$l= 1;
do {
$w++;
$l++;
$area = $w * $l;
} while ($area < 1000);
```

echo "The smallest square over 1000 sq. ft in area is $w ft. x $l ft.";

? >

In this example, the code inside the loop will run before the condition is tested. What this means is that the variable *$area* will at least have a value before we arrive at the testing phase. Now, if the area will continue to have a value of less than 1000, then the loop will continue to run.

The 'for' loop

So far you have learned about the while, and the 'do while' loop. But, there is one other type of loop that's more compact and neat, the 'for' loop. I would suggest that you use the 'for' loop when you have a specific number in your head which you want the loop to repeat. With the 'for' loop, you can create a counter variable which will record the number of loops. The syntax for a 'loop' is:

for (expression1; exression2; expression3) {

// run the code

}

// Additional code goes here

Looking at the above syntax, we realize that unlike the 'do while' loops which only have one expression in their parenthesis, the 'for loop' has three expressions. The expressions are described below in order:

- **Initializer**

This runs only once. The 'for' statement initializes a counter first.

- **Loop test**

This has the same function as the single expression in the 'do while' loop. So, if the expression test is true, then the loop continues, but if it is false, then the loop exits.

- **Counting**

This is used to change the value of the counter

The code snippet below is a demonstration of the 'for loop.' Kindly study it:

```
for ($1=1; $1<= 10; $1++) {

echo "I have reached: $1 <br />";

}

echo "finished";
```

This example shows how efficient a 'for loop' can be.

Loops and the break statement

When you are working with the 'do while' and many others, the loop will run until the point it is found to be false.

But, it is possible to exit a loop while it's in the middle by applying the 'break' statement. This operates the same way it does inside a switch construct.

Why should you break from this loop? Well, in some instances it is still right to exit out of the loop. For example, the infinite 'for' loop will continue to run and run until it exhausts the resources on the server.

Another reason why you might want to exit a loop is when you have completed doing whatever kind of process you wanted to achieve.

Creating nested loops

Have you ever heard of a loop within a loop? Below is an example of how a 'nested' loop will look:

```
for ($t = 0; $t < 10; $t++) {
for ($u = 0; $u < 10; $u++) {
echo $t. $u. "< br / >";
}
}
```

Strings

When it comes to programming, a string is a series of characters. For example, 'many,' 'how are you,' and 'morning' are all valid strings. In essence, the web is entirely made up of a string of data. HTML and XHTML comprise of strings. This part will take you through some of the crucial things you need to be aware of regarding strings in PHP.

Creating and accessing strings

To create a string variable is very simple, all it takes is to initialize your variable with a literal string value. For instance:

```
$yourstring= 'hello';
```

If you check the example above, the literal string is enclosed in single quotes. But, you can still use the double quotation marks. Something which you need to note is that both single and double quotation marks operate differently. A string enclosed with single quotation marks lets PHP use it exactly as it has been typed.

Here, the double quotation marks have several additional features:

- You can use special characters
- You can parse and replace

Create a string using this method

Earlier, I had taught you how you can create a string, but there are different other ways as shown in the examples below:

$yourstring= $mystring;

$yourstring = "how". "are". "you?";

$yourstring = ($x > 200)? "Bigger number": "Smaller number";

Length of a string

The function *strlen ()* will help you determine the length of a string. The function accepts the string value as the argument and outputs the length of the string. For example:

$yourstring= "goalpost";

echo strlen ($yourstring). "<br/>"; // outputs 8

Gaining access to string characters

Do you want to learn how you can access individual characters in a string?

PHP offers you with an easy approach. Study this example to learn:

$character = $string[index];

Arrays

At this point, you already know what a variable is in PHP. We said that a variable is a container which can hold a single value. However, there are specific types of variables which can store more than one value. An example of that variable is the array, and the other one is the object.

Arrays are an incredible feature in programming languages because it gives one the ability to work with huge sizes of data. As an excellent form of data storage, the two major properties of arrays are:

- An array has no fixed size, which means it can store millions of values

- It is very simple to manipulate multiple array values all at once

To begin with, let's first define an array.

Arrays are simply a unique form of a variable with added functionality. For example, arrays will help you store as many values in just one variable. Let's say, for example, you have a lot of soccer balls which you would like to store. If you want to store all your balls in a single variable, this is how your piece of code will look like:

$ball1= "Map";

$ball2=" Success";

$ball3 = "Mountains";

Assume, now that you have a list of books.

$book1= "Map";

$book2=" Success";

$book3 = "Mountains";

Well, suppose you wanted to loop through your list of books and pick one? Or let's assume that you don't have 3 books but 400? The best tactic to use here is the array. An array allows you to store all your books in one single variable name. Plus, you can access the array by using the array name.

In an array, each element stored has its own index to ensure that the process of accessing it becomes simple. PHP has three types of arrays, and we are going to discuss each type one by one.

Numeric array

This is an array that has a numeric index. A numeric array assigns each array element a numeric index.

To create a numeric array, you can use two methods:

- In this first example, the index is automatically assigned:

  $books = array ("Tom and Mary", "The happy ending", "The Storm");

- In this second example, the index is assigned manually:

  $books [0] = "Tom and Mary";

  $books [1] = "The happy ending";

  $books [2] = "The Storm";

Associative arrays

In this array, we will link the key with the value stored. But, when you want to store the type of data related to individual values, a numeric array is never the best to use. Instead, an associative array is the best option to go with.

This example uses an array to assign the age of various people:

$ages = array ("David" =>22, "Peter" => 40, "Steve" =>37);

You can then use the ID keys in a script like:

<? php

$ages['David'] = "22"; $ages['Peter'] = "40"; $ages['Steve'] = "34"; echo "Peter is ". $ages['Peter']. " years old. ";?>

This code will display Peter is 40 years old.

Multidimensional arrays

When it comes to the multidimensional array, each element is an array. So, it is like we have an array of arrays. In the example below, we have created a multidimensional array with ID keys:

$class=array

(

"Geoffrey" =>array

(

"Meghan",

"Eden",

"Hazard"

),

"Jameson" =>array

(

"Mike"

),

"White" =>array

(

"Cleveland",

"Edwin",

"Junior"

)

);

This array would look this if written together with the output:

Array

(

[Geoffrey]=>Array

(

[0]=>Meghan

[1]=>Eden

[2]=>Hazard

)

[Jameson]=>Array

(

[0]=>Mike

)

[White]=>Array

(

[0]=>Cleveland

[1]=>Edwin

[2]=>Junior

)

)

If we want to display a single value from one of the arrays above, then we do that by using the following code:

echo "does". $class['Geoffrey'][2]. "belong to the Geoffrey class?";

This code will display the following: "does Eden belong to the Geoffrey class?"

Functions

A function is a block of code which performs a specific task. A function is defined by following a certain syntax, and then you can call the function from a different section of your code. The syntax that you should follow whenever you are creating a PHP function is:

function nameOfFunction ()

{

//Script to be executed

}

When creating PHP functions, one is always advised to give the function a name which corresponds to the task the function is going to do. The name of the function can even begin with an underscore or a letter, but it should start with a number. Here is an example of a function which will ask for my name:

<? php

Function Askname ()

{

echo "What is your name?"

}

echo "Please, ";

Askname ();

?>

The script will display the following: *"Please, what is your name?"*

Function parameters in PHP

If we want to increase the functionality of the function, then we need to add more parameters. You can look at a parameter as a variable. Parameters appear inside the function parenthesis. Look at the example below which uses parameters, the function is going to print several first names, but it will still retain the last names:

```php
<? php function showName($fname) {

echo $fname. " Rael. <br />";

}

echo "My name is ";

showName ("Kai Jam");

echo "My brother's name is ";

showName("Hoda");

echo "My cousin's name is ";

showName("Stuart") ;>
```

See the output below:

My name is Kai Jam Rael.
My brother's name is Hoda Rael.
My cousin's name is Stuart Rael.

In this example, the function *showName ()* has one parameter. It is still possible for a function to have more than one parameter.

Return values in PHP

If you want a function in PHP to return a value. We simply apply the 'return' statement. Consider this example:

```php
<? php function sum($x,$y) {

$total=$x+$y;

return $total;

}
echo "3 + 6 = ". sum (3,6);

?>
```

The output of this code will be 3 + 6 = 7

Chapter 3

PHP Form Handling

So far, you are now familiar with the basics of PHP and the way the PHP program works. You have also learned some of the core basics of the PHP language. I am sure you can declare a variable, write a PHP function, and many other important things which a person knowledgeable with PHP is supposed to know. From this point on, you will learn how to build practical PHP applications. One of the most popular capabilities of PHP is the ability to receive input entered by a visitor through an application. The previous scripts which we have done don't actually allow a user to enter values. However, if you can add that feature where a user can enter some values and read the input, then your PHP program becomes more interactive.

A common practice is letting the visitor of a web application enter some data is by using the HTML form. I know you have filled in a lot of HTML forms. Popular HTML forms include the contact form and order forms where you can order products from an online shop.

User input and PHP forms

The $\_POST$ and $\_GET$ are the two main methods used in PHP to get information from forms. The most important thing which you need to note down is that, whenever you are handling HTML forms together with PHP, all HTML form elements will also be present in your PHP code snippets.

This example has an HTML form and a submit button:

```
<html>

<body>

<form action=" home. Php" method=" post">

Your Name: <input type="text" name="firstname"/>

Your age: <input type="text" name="age"/>

<input type="Submit"/>

<form>

</body>

</html>
```

If the user submits the above form after entering the data, the form goes to the *home.php* file. The output of this form could be something like: "Welcome Mike! You are 30 years old."

Let's turn our attention to the PHP form validation. Whenever a user has entered data and clicked 'send,' it is important for the data to be validated by the client code. You can still perform browser validation. In fact, the browser validation is faster and reduces the server load.

However, if you are going to store your data in a database, it is recommended that you perform server validation. The best method to go with server validation is to post the form to the same page. Don't go to a different page. By doing this, you will help the user see the error message while they're in the same form.

$_GET is a built-in function which will help you collect values from a form using the method 'get.'

The Function $_GET

We use the built-in *$_GET* function to gather values from a form using the method GET. When you use the GET method, any information that is sent will be visible to everyone. The information will be displayed in the address bar of the browser. In addition, there are limits to the amount of information you can send.

So, when is it applicable to use the method get?

First, if you are fine with all of your variable names and values appearing in the URL, then you can use the method 'get.' But, you should never send your most sensitive data using this method. Again, large quantities of information are unfit for this method.

The $_POST Function

The *$_POST* function is another function which can be used in the PHP forms to collect values from a form after it has been sent from the method 'post.' The greatest thing with this method is that it provides security for your data. Nobody can see the information which you are sending. In addition, there is no restriction on the amount of data which you can send. However, an 8MB max size is the default size for the post, but still, you can change this on the *post_max_size* in your *php.in* file.

```
<form action="welcome.php" method="post">
Name: <input type="text" name="fname" />
Age: <input type="text" name="age" />
<input type="submit" />
</form>
```

When the data is submitted in the example above. This is how the URL will look:

"http://www.example.com/welcome.php"

The $_REQUEST Function

This function holds the details of the *$_POST, $_GET* as well as the *$_COOKIE*.

The *$_REQUEST* is a powerful function since it combines both the post and get. Before we can close this topic on form handling, it is also important to talk about the URL redirection. While it might not be related to the forms in a direct manner, URL redirection is something which you may have interacted with more than once. This is something you usually encounter when you fill out online forms.

Another helpful thing you can get by using the redirect feature is that you eliminate the possibility of users resubmitting the form when they reload the browser page. Instead, they refresh the page that they have been redirected to.

If you want to redirect your users to a given page, it will be very simple. No stress involved. All you need to do is write: *Location: HTTP header*, plus the URL you want to redirect.

The example below explains everything.

header ("Location: thankyou.html");

Chapter 4

Introduction Databases and SQL

Making a decision about the way you store your data

As a developer, you need to note that when you start building applications which require you to store data, you must know which method your application will use to store the data. To help you make this decision. Here are some things that you should think of:

- The people who will access the data

- How much will the size be after, let's say, 10 years?

- What is the limit of my data?

- Will my application access the data frequently?

- The frequency of updates you may need to perform.

Once you have considered the above points, then you need to make a decision on which approach you are going to use.

A database management engine is the most popular model used when you want to store, modify, and retrieve data.

Database architectures

Before we can get started with the database topic, there are two options for database architecture which you can pick: a client-server and the embedded model.

An embedded database exists within the application which needs it. This means it runs on the same machine as the application host. In addition, it stores the data in the same host application machine.

Client-server models on, the other hand, these are flexible and powerful databases. Mostly, they are applied in networks. Database models come in two types:

- **Simple database model**

A simple type of database similar to an associative data array. Every data item is referenced using a single key. In this model, it is difficult to create a relationship between the data stored in the database.

- **Relational databases**

This gives one enormous ability and flexibility. It is among the most popular options. You will find that the relational database is common in the web sector. If you have ever heard someone mention RDBMS, then this is what they were referring to. Some examples of RDBMS in PHP include *PostgreSQL & MySQL*.

For this chapter, we will be focusing on the MySQL. The MySQL database model gives one of the following advantages:

- It is very popular across the web

- It is cheap and available in a majority of the web hosting accounts

- Very simple to use

- It is powerful, fast and can handle large complex data

- It is very easy to install, no complex steps to follow

- It can be installed for free

Relational databases in depth

As the name suggests, a relational database will offer the ability for data to be associated and categorized using certain attributes. For example, a record of students can be grouped by age, height, or date. In a relational database, data is organized in a table of rows and columns.

This is an example of a database table:

playerNumber	name	phoneNumber	datePlayed	nickname
42	David	555-1234	03/03/04	Dodge
6	Nic	555-3456	03/03/04	Obi-d
2	David	555-6543	03/03/04	Witblitz
14	Mark	555-1213	03/03/04	Greeny
2	David	555-6543	02/25/04	Witblitz
25	Pads	555-9101	02/25/04	Pads
6	Nic	555-3456	02/25/04	Obi-d
7	Nic	555-5678	02/25/04	Nicrot

In the table above, you should be able to identify the rows and columns. You will see that the rows hold information about every player while the columns are identified with a heading. This is called the column name or field name.

Normalization

In this table, you will notice that any time there is a match, all the details of a player have to be written down. It does not matter whether the details already exist or not. The end result is time wasting and repetition. Repetition of the same information such as the players' phone number is referred to as redundancy. Redundancy is unacceptable in a database. It wastes a lot of space and time.

Preventing redundancy is called 'normalization.' For instance, if we are to normalize the above table, we need to create another table for *playernumber*, *name*, *phonenumber,* and *nickname*. The table will look like this:

playerNumber	name	phoneNumber	nickname
42	David	555-1234	Dodge
6	Nic	555-3456	Obi-d
14	Mark	555-1213	Greeny
2	David	555-6543	Witblitz
25	Pads	555-9101	Pads
7	Nic	555-5678	Nicrot

You will now notice that on this table, each player only has one record. The player number is the unique field which identifies every player. Now that we have removed part of the players' information, we will create another table with the remaining details:

playerNumber	datePlayed
42	03/03/04
6	03/03/04
2	03/03/04
14	03/03/04
2	02/25/04
25	02/25/04
6	02/25/04
7	02/25/04

In this table, we have the *playerNumber* retained because it is the unique field which identifies each player. Now, if we can link up this second table and the previous one using the unique field, we can successfully associate a player and the date they played a match. In this example, we now say that the two tables are linked together using the *playerNumber* field. The *playerNumber* field in this last table is called the 'foreign key' because it points to the primary key in the previous table.

If you look at the above case, the only repeating information is the *playerNumber*. Therefore, we have saved a lot of space and time compared to the original table where we had to write all of the information. This type of relation is called 'one, too many' relations. This is because a single record of a player can be related to many other records if the player plays more than one game. The whole process that we have done is called normalization.

SQL

SQL is an acronym that stands for structured query language. SQL gives you the ability to carry out any operation related to the database such as creating a database and many other tasks. Even though this chapter focuses on MySQL, we will also mention SQL since it is another version of MySQL. But, because the basics of SQL are similar to MySQL, then you can apply them to MySQL.

MySQL Data types

Any time you create a MySQL data type, you must specify the type and size of every field. The data types in MySQL include numeric, string, and date.

The numeric types of data

Numeric Data Type	Description	Allowed Range of Values
TINYINT	Very small integer	–128 to 127, or 0 to 255 if UNSIGNED
SMALLINT	Small integer	–32768 to 32767, or 0 to 65535 if UNSIGNED
MEDIUMINT	Medium-sized integer	–8388608 to 8388607, or 0 to 16777215 if UNSIGNED
INT	Normal-sized integer	–2147483648 to 2147483647, or 0 to 4294967295 if UNSIGNED
BIGINT	Large integer	–9223372036854775808 to 9223372036854775807, or 0 to 18446744073709551615 if UNSIGNED
FLOAT	Single-precision floating-point number	Smallest non-zero value: $\pm1.176 \times 10^{-38}$; largest value: $\pm3.403 \times 10^{38}$
DOUBLE	Double-precision floating-point number	Smallest non-zero value: $\pm2.225 \times 10^{-308}$; largest value: $\pm1.798 \times 10^{308}$
DECIMAL(precision, scale)	Fixed-point number	Same as DOUBLE, but fixed-point rather than floating-point. precision specifies the total number of allowed digits, whereas scale specifies how many digits sit to the right of the decimal point.
BIT	0 or 1	0 or 1

Date and time data types

Date/Time Data Type	Description	Allowed Range of Values
DATE	Date	1 Jan 1000 to 31 Dec 9999
DATETIME	Date and time	Midnight, 1 Jan 1000 to 23:59:59, 31 Dec 9999
TIMESTAMP	Timestamp	00:00:01, 1 Jan 1970 to 03:14:07, 9 Jan 2038, UTC (Universal Coordinated Time)
TIME	Time	–838:59:59 to 838:59:59
YEAR	Year	1901 to 2155

String data types

String Data Type	Description	Allowed Lengths
CHAR(n)	Fixed-length string of n characters	0–255 characters
VARCHAR(n)	Variable-length string of up to n characters	0–65535 characters
BINARY(n)	Fixed-length binary string of n bytes	0–255 bytes
VARBINARY(n)	Variable-length binary string of up to n bytes	0–65535 bytes
TINYTEXT	Small text field	0–255 characters
TEXT	Normal-sized text field	0–65535 characters
MEDIUMTEXT	Medium-sized text field	0–16777215 characters
LONGTEXT	Large text field	0–4294967295 characters
TINYBLOB	Small BLOB (Binary Large Object)	0–255 bytes
BLOB	Normal-sized BLOB	0–65535 bytes
MEDIUMBLOB	Medium-sized BLOB	0–16777215 bytes (16MB)
LONGBLOB	Large BLOB	0–4294967295 bytes (4GB)
ENUM	Enumeration	The field can contain one value from a predefined list of up to 65,535 values
SET	A set of values	The field can contain zero or more values from a predefined list of up to 64 values

SQL Statements

To succeed in working with databases and tables, you must learn and know how to apply SQL statements. Popular SQL statements include:

- SELECT

- UPDATE

- REPLACE

- INSERT

- DELETE

Other statements include:

- CREATE

- DROP

- ALTER

Connecting to MySQL using PHP

Well, now you are familiar with the MySQL database terms. We can now take you through a brief study of connecting your database with MYSQL. There are two ways which you can use PHP to connect to the MYSQL database:

- MySQLi (MYSQL improved)

- PDO (PHP Data Objects)

As you can see, the existence of the two methods points that each method has an advantage and a disadvantage. Which one is the best could just lead to an endless debate which we might never finish. In this book, we are going to use the MySQLi method.

The MySQL improved extension has the MySQLi class. To connect your database using PHP, follow the steps below:

1. You will require your MySQL server address. However, if the database exists on the same server, it will possibly be the local host.

2. Create a PHP file name, and you can name it as *connect.php.*

3. Type the PHP code below in your *connect.php* file. Make sure that you replace the username, password, and *dname* with your own details:

```php
<?php

$mysqli= new mysqli ("localhost", "username", "password", "dname");

?>
```

4. Once the code has connected to the MYSQL, you can move on by selecting your database. You can also run SQL queries and do other operations that you want.

Retrieving data using 'select'

One of the most interesting things with the databases is the speed at which you can retrieve data in whatever order you want. Consider it as a database which stores books. If you want to display the contents of the database organized by the last and first name, SQL can help you achieve this quickly by using the ORDER BY statement:

"SELECT username, firstname, lastname FROM books ORDER BY firstname;"

Summarizing data

MySQL gives you the ability to summarize data instead of just presenting the actual data stored in the database. Use the following functions to summarize your data:

- *Sum()*

- *Avg()*

- *Max()*

- *Count ()*

Chapter 5

Manipulate MySQL Data With PHP

Inserting records

The SQL statement INSERT INTO helps one place records into a database table:

INSERT INTO name of table VALUES (v1, v2....);

If you only want to insert specific values, letting the remaining fields become nulls, you can use:

INSERT INTO name of table (field1, field2, ...) VALUES (v1, v2, ...);

To insert data into a table using PHP, first, we need to use the INSERT INTO statement and write the SQL query with the required values. The basic SQL INSERT INTO looks this way:

INSERT [INTO] name of the table (names of column) VALUES (values)

The square brackets around INTO are optional. It serves as a way to improve readability. The column names can be placed in any order. But, the values in the parenthesis must appear exactly as in the columns.

The picture below has a code snippet of how the INSERT INTO is used:

```
01.  <?php
02.  /* Attempt MySQL server connection. Assuming you are running MySQL
03.  server with default setting (user 'root' with no password) */
04.  $link = mysqli_connect("localhost", "root", "", "demo");
05.
06.  // Check connection
07.  if($link === false){
08.      die("ERROR: Could not connect. " . mysqli_connect_error());
09.  }
10.
11.  // Attempt insert query execution
12.  $sql = "INSERT INTO persons (first_name, last_name, email) VALUES ('Peter',
         'Parker', 'peterparker@mail.com')";
13.  if(mysqli_query($link, $sql)){
14.      echo "Records inserted successfully.";
15.  } else{
16.      echo "ERROR: Could not able to execute $sql. " . mysqli_error($link);
17.  }
18.
19.  // Close connection
20.  mysqli_close($link);
21.  ?>
```

We have to connect to the database first. Once the connection is done, the INSERT statement is executed. In this code, we are injecting data into a table of persons. The values we are inserting are the *fname, lname,* and email.

Once the records have been successfully inserted, a message will be displayed on the screen to inform us that the process has been successful. In case the process of inserting the records fails, an error message will be shown on the screen. Something else which you need to pay attention to is the way we have used the 'if, else' statement which we learned at the start of this book.

Insertion in multiple rows

SQL is a useful language which can allow you to perform the insertion of many rows into a database table by writing a single line of query.

In this example, we have added more rows to the table:

```php
<?php
/* Attempt MySQL server connection. Assuming you are running MySQL
server with default setting (user 'root' with no password) */
$link = mysqli_connect("localhost", "root", "", "demo");

// Check connection
if($link === false){
    die("ERROR: Could not connect. " . mysqli_connect_error());
}

// Attempt insert query execution
$sql = "INSERT INTO persons (first_name, last_name, email) VALUES
            ('John', 'Rambo', 'johnrambo@mail.com'),
            ('Clark', 'Kent', 'clarkkent@mail.com'),
            ('John', 'Carter', 'johncarter@mail.com'),
            ('Harry', 'Potter', 'harrypotter@mail.com')";
if(mysqli_query($link, $sql)){
    echo "Records added successfully.";
} else{
    echo "ERROR: Could not able to execute $sql. " . mysqli_error($link);
}

// Close connection
mysqli_close($link);
?>
```

Looking at the above example, you can see that every row is distinguished by a comma and surrounded with parenthesis.

Records update

The update statement is another useful statement which will let you make changes to the data stored in the table. We use the update statement together with the WHERE clause.

The basic form of an UPDATE statement looks like this:

"UPDATE table_name SET c1= value, c2 = value2, ...WHERE column_name=yourvalue"

Something you should always remember is that whenever you update a table, make sure you can tell the primary key. A practical approach to this is writing a query to the database and indicating all the records. After this, you can show these results together with a link to the update page.

50

But, for now, let's create a SQL query that has the UPDATE statement and the WHERE construct. After we have done this, we will move on to execute the query by passing the query to a *mysqli_query ()* function which completes the update function.

In our update statement, we want to update the table person's email address if the person in the 'person table' has an id of 1:

```
01.  <?php
02.  /* Attempt MySQL server connection. Assuming you are running MySQL
03.  server with default setting (user 'root' with no password) */
04.  $link = mysqli_connect("localhost", "root", "", "demo");
05.
06.  // Check connection
07.  if($link === false){
08.      die("ERROR: Could not connect. " . mysqli_connect_error());
09.  }
10.
11.  // Attempt update query execution
12.  $sql = "UPDATE persons SET email='peterparker_new@mail.com' WHERE id=1";
13.  if(mysqli_query($link, $sql)){
14.      echo "Records were updated successfully.";
15.  } else {
16.      echo "ERROR: Could not able to execute $sql. " . mysqli_error($link);
17.  }
18.
19.  // Close connection
20.  mysqli_close($link);
21.  ?>
```

As you can see, we establish a connection first with the database. Once the connection is successful, our UPDATE statement is the next to be executed.

Deleting a record

In the same way, you can update and insert records into a table. You can also delete the same values in the table with the help of the SQL statement. And don't forget that the DELETE statement is also used together with the WHERE construct to delete all records which fulfill a given condition. The DELETE construct is as follows:

DELETE FROM tble_name WHERE condition

However, something which you need to be careful with when using the DELETE command is that it is final. The moment a record is deleted, it will never be recovered. The record is gone forever. Don't confuse this with your computer where you have a recycle bin to go and restore your records. No! The action is permanent. The worst thing with this DELETE syntax is that the WHERE construct is optional. This means if you fail to put it in your code, every record is going to be deleted, and you will never recover it unless you have a backup. So, whenever you have to write the delete command, instead of the process being instant, you should display the records which you want to be deleted to the user to confirm everything first before you perform the deletion process.

Now, we can get into the practical side. In the picture below, the PHP code will delete the records of all those persons whose first name on the table is equivalent to John:

```
01.  <?php
02.  /* Attempt MySQL server connection. Assuming you are running MySQL
03.  server with default setting (user 'root' with no password) */
04.  $link = mysqli_connect("localhost", "root", "", "demo");
05.
06.  // Check connection
07.  if($link === false){
08.      die("ERROR: Could not connect. " . mysqli_connect_error());
09.  }
10.
11.  // Attempt delete query execution
12.  $sql = "DELETE FROM persons WHERE first_name='John'";
13.  if(mysqli_query($link, $sql)){
14.      echo "Records were deleted successfully.";
15.  } else{
16.      echo "ERROR: Could not able to execute $sql. " . mysqli_error($link);
17.  }
18.
19.  // Close connection
20.  mysqli_close($link);
21.  ?>
```

Building a member registration application

In this section, I'll walk you through the steps of building a user registration application. The registration system will give users the ability to create an account by providing details such as their username, password, email and they can also sign out if needed. Also, you will learn how you can use PHP to restrict users from certain pages. In short, this practical application will make use of all the concepts we have learned in each of the chapters in this book.

First, let's set up our database

Now, I want you to create a database and assign it your favorite name. I will call my database 'registration.' As I said at the start, always try to give your variables, databases, and so forth, names which relate to the operation or function you want to do. Our registration database will have a table called 'users.' Our 'users table' has the following fields:

- Email

- Username

- Password

- User id

Below is the picture of my table:

If you are not happy using the PHPMYADMIN wizard, you can go with the MySQL prompt. Just type the commands below:

```
CREATE TABLE `users` (
  `id` int(11) NOT NULL AUTO_INCREMENT PRIMARY KEY,
  `username` varchar(100) NOT NULL,
  `email` varchar(100) NOT NULL,
  `password` varchar(100) NOT NULL
) ENGINE=InnoDB DEFAULT CHARSET=latin1;
```

If you have successfully done that, then well done! You have successfully created a database. The next thing I would like you to do is to create a folder inside the root directory of your server. I want to assume that you are using WAMPP or XAMPP as your localhost. Locate the folder called *htcdocs* and create the folder inside it. Once you are done creating the registration folder, I want you to create the following files inside the registration folder:

- errors.php

- index.php

- login.php

- server.php

- style.css

If you have done that, open your files in your best editor. I am using Sublime Text 3.

User registration

```php
<?php include('server.php') ?>
<!DOCTYPE html>
<html>
<head>
    <title>Registration system PHP and MySQL</title>
    <link rel="stylesheet" type="text/css" href="style.css">
</head>
<body>
    <div class="header">
        <h2>Register</h2>
    </div>

    <form method="post" action="register.php">
        <?php include('errors.php'); ?>
        <div class="input-group">
            <label>Username</label>
            <input type="text" name="username" value="<?php echo $username; ?>">
        </div>
        <div class="input-group">
            <label>Email</label>
            <input type="email" name="email" value="<?php echo $email; ?>">
        </div>
        <div class="input-group">
            <label>Password</label>
            <input type="password" name="password_1">
        </div>
        <div class="input-group">
            <label>Confirm password</label>
            <input type="password" name="password_2">
        </div>
        <div class="input-group">
            <button type="submit" class="btn" name="reg_user">Register</button>
        </div>
        <p>
            Already a member? <a href="login.php">Sign in</a>
        </p>
    </form>
</body>
</html>
```

Go to the *register.php* file in your text editor. You can either copy and paste the code below or type it.

This picture shows an HTML form. But, some of the things which you need to note is the method 'action' which has been assigned to the *register.php*. What this one means is that when the user selects the

55

register button, all the data contained in the form will go back to the same page. If you can still remember, when I was talking about the PHP form handling I did recommend that you apply this technique. At the top of this same page, I have included the *server.php* because some of this data is going to be received by the server.

You should also be able to recognize that we have included the *errors.php* file as a way to show errors from the form. Something else which you should see is that we are using the 'post' and not the 'get' method because we don't want anyone to see our information. Remember that we will be submitting data which has a password. Plus, the 'post' method works for data of just about any size.

Also, in the header section, we have put *CSS* links. There is a style sheet called *style.css*. I believe you already understand the role of *CSS*. So, open your *style.css* file and type the code below:

```css
* {
  margin: 0px;
  padding: 0px;
}
body {
  font-size: 120%;
  background: #F8F8FF;
}

.header {
  width: 30%;
  margin: 50px auto 0px;
  color: white;
  background: #5F9EA0;
  text-align: center;
  border: 1px solid #80C4DE;
  border-bottom: none;
  border-radius: 10px 10px 0px 0px;
  padding: 20px;
}
```

```css
form, .content {
  width: 30%;
  margin: 0px auto;
  padding: 20px;
  border: 1px solid #B0C4DE;
  background: white;
  border-radius: 0px 0px 10px 10px;
}
.input-group {
  margin: 10px 0px 10px 0px;
}
.input-group label {
  display: block;
  text-align: left;
  margin: 3px;
}
.input-group input {
  height: 30px;
  width: 93%;
  padding: 5px 10px;
  font-size: 16px;
  border-radius: 5px;
  border: 1px solid gray;
}
```

```css
.btn {
    padding: 10px;
    font-size: 15px;
    color: white;
    background: #5F9EA0;
    border: none;
    border-radius: 5px;
}
.error {
    width: 92%;
    margin: 0px auto;
    padding: 10px;
    border: 1px solid #a94442;
    color: #a94442;
    background: #f2dede;
    border-radius: 5px;
    text-align: left;
}
.success {
    color: #3c763d;
    background: #dff0d8;
    border: 1px solid #3c763d;
    margin-bottom: 20px;
}
```

By using the *CSS*, the form will look very beautiful. Now, it is time to write the script which is going to collect the information submitted from the HTML form and store it in the database. This is going to be completed in the *server.php*. So, go and open the *server.php* then type in the following code:

```php
<?php
session_start();

// initializing variables
$username = "";
$email    = "";
$errors = array();

// connect to the database
$db = mysqli_connect("localhost", 'root', '', 'registration');

// REGISTER USER
if (isset($_POST['reg_user'])) {
  // receive all input values from the form
  $username = mysqli_real_escape_string($db, $_POST['username']);
  $email = mysqli_real_escape_string($db, $_POST['email']);
  $password_1 = mysqli_real_escape_string($db, $_POST['password_1']);
  $password_2 = mysqli_real_escape_string($db, $_POST['password_2']);

  // form validation: ensure that the form is correctly filled ...
  // by adding (array_push()) corresponding error unto $errors array
  if (empty($username)) { array_push($errors, "Username is required"); }
  if (empty($email)) { array_push($errors, "Email is required"); }
  if (empty($password_1)) { array_push($errors, "Password is required"); }
  if ($password_1 != $password_2) {
    array_push($errors, "The two passwords do not match");
  }

  // first check the database to make sure
  // a user does not already exist with the same username and/or email
  $user_check_query = "SELECT * FROM users WHERE username='$username' OR email='$email' LIMIT 1";
  $result = mysqli_query($db, $user_check_query);
  $user = mysqli_fetch_assoc($result);

  if ($user) { // if user exists
    if ($user['username'] === $username) {
      array_push($errors, "Username already exists");
    }

    if ($user['email'] === $email) {
      array_push($errors, "email already exists");
    }
  }

  // Finally, register user if there are no errors in the form
  if (count($errors) == 0) {
    $password = md5($password_1);//encrypt the password before saving in the database

    $query = "INSERT INTO users (username, email, password)
          VALUES('$username', '$email', '$password')";
    mysqli_query($db, $query);
    $_SESSION['username'] = $username;
    $_SESSION['success'] = "You are now logged in";
    header('location: index.php');
  }
}

// ...
```

In this code, we are using sessions help track the users. A session is started by creating the *session_start()* at the top of the file. The comments in the code try to explain everything that is happening. However, there are a few things which I would like to talk about.

The 'if statement' helps determine whether or not the *reg_user* button located on the registration form has been clicked. Don't forget that if you go to our form, specifically on the submit button, the name attribute assigned to it is the *reg_user* which is the one being referenced to in the 'if statement.'

All data submitted from the form has to be analyzed to confirm that whatever the user entered was correct. Passwords have to be checked to ensure that they match. If the user keyed in every detail, then this means that there are no mistakes when the form is submitted. The details of the user will be successfully entered into the 'users' table. This way, the user registration would be successfully completed. Another important point to pay attention to is that the password entered into the 'users' table will be hashed. This means it will be secured so that no one can tamper with it. An advantage which comes with hashing your password is, if a hacker gains entry into your database, they will not manage to read your password.

In our current code, you can't see the error messages because we haven't written the *error.php* code. Well, if you want to display errors, type the following code into the *error.php* file:

```php
<?php if (count($errors) > 0) : ?>
  <div class="error">
    <?php foreach ($errors as $error) : ?>
      <p><?php echo $error ?></p>
    <?php endforeach ?>
  </div>
<?php endif ?>
```

In our registration page, we have created it in such a way that whenever a user successfully registers, the application will take them straight to the page called *index.php*.

Now, let's examine the user login. If there is something that's quite easy to build, it's the login page. Just open your text editor and type the code below:

```
1  <?php include('server.php') ?>
2  <!DOCTYPE html>
3  <html>
4  <head>
5    <title>Registration system PHP and MySQL</title>
6    <link rel="stylesheet" type="text/css" href="style.css">
7  </head>
8  <body>
9    <div class="header">
10     <h2>Login</h2>
11   </div>
12
13   <form method="post" action="login.php">
14     <?php include('errors.php'); ?>
15     <div class="input-group">
16       <label>Username</label>
17       <input type="text" name="username" >
18     </div>
19     <div class="input-group">
20       <label>Password</label>
21       <input type="password" name="password">
22     </div>
23     <div class="input-group">
24       <button type="submit" class="btn" name="login_user">Login</button>
25     </div>
26     <p>
27       Not yet a member? <a href="register.php">Sign up</a>
28     </p>
29   </form>
30 </body>
31 </html>
```

Most of the things in this code resemble what was on the *register.php* page.

Now, when it comes to writing the code that will sign in the user, we have to do that in the *server.php*. So, open your *server.php* code and type this code at the end of the file:

```
// LOGIN USER
if (isset($_POST['login_user'])) {
  $username = mysqli_real_escape_string($db, $_POST['username']);
  $password = mysqli_real_escape_string($db, $_POST['password']);

  if (empty($username)) {
    array_push($errors, "Username is required");
  }
  if (empty($password)) {
    array_push($errors, "Password is required");
  }

  if (count($errors) == 0) {
    $password = md5($password);
    $query = "SELECT * FROM users WHERE username='$username' AND password='$password'";
    $results = mysqli_query($db, $query);
    if (mysqli_num_rows($results) == 1) {
      $_SESSION['username'] = $username;
      $_SESSION['success'] = "You are now logged in";
      header('location: index.php');
    } else {
      array_push($errors, "Wrong username/password combination");
    }
  }
}
?>
```

Again, what this code does is that it checks whether or not the user has entered data in all the fields correctly and verify that all the credentials which were provided matched with the ones stored in the database. If they match the code, then it will log them in. Once the user is signed in already, they will be directed to the page where they will be told that they were logged in successfully.

Now, it is time to find out what is going on in the *index.php* file. Open the file and type in the following code:

62

```php
        <?php endif ?>

        <!-- logged in user information -->
        <?php if (isset($_SESSION['username'])) : ?>
            <p>Welcome <strong><?php echo $_SESSION['username']; ?></strong></p>
            <p> <a href="index.php?logout='1'" style="color: red;">logout</a> </p>
        <?php endif ?>
    </div>

    </body>
    </html>


    <?php
      session_start();

      if (!isset($_SESSION['username'])) {
        $_SESSION['msg'] = "You must log in first";
        header('location: login.php');
      }
      if (isset($_GET['logout'])) {
        session_destroy();
        unset($_SESSION['username']);
        header("location: login.php");
      }
    ?>
    <!DOCTYPE html>
    <html>
    <head>
      <title>Home</title>
      <link rel="stylesheet" type="text/css" href="style.css">
    </head>
    <body>

    <div class="header">
      <h2>Home Page</h2>
    </div>
    <div class="content">
        <!-- notification message -->
        <?php if (isset($_SESSION['success'])) : ?>
          <div class="error success" >
            <h3>
              <?php
                echo $_SESSION['success'];
                unset($_SESSION['success']);
              ?>
            </h3>
          </div>
```

In this code, we use the 'if clause statement' to check if the user signed in already. If they're not logged in yet, they will be taken to the login interface. This means that this page is only visible to users who are already logged in. Now, if you want to make certain pages accessible only to the users who have logged in, all it takes is to have this snippet of code appear at the top of the file.

In the second 'if' statement, we want to check if the user has already clicked the 'sign out' button. If it is evaluated as 'true,' the user is then logged out and taken back to the main page to log in. If you have done everything up to this point, then try to run your whole application. Attempt to register yourself as the new user. You can now personalize this site so that it suits your needs.

Chapter 6

PHP Sessions, Cookies, and Authentication

As you continue to build your web projects, there are complicated applications which will require you to monitor your visitors and users. You may not have built a login system, but you might need some certain details of your users. Some of these details could be the sessions of your users.

Different technologies have been created to help you accomplish this. Some of these technologies include browser cookies and HTTP authentication. These technologies will allow you to monitor your visitors through the use of a seamless process.

PHP Cookies

A cookie is a data object which a web server will store on your hard drive using the web browser. It can have any kind of alphanumeric information as long as it does not exceed 4KB, and it can be recovered from your computer and taken back to the server. Some of the popular uses of cookies include tracking session of users, storing the shipping cart, storing data from different visits, holding login details, and other functions.

Cookies are a private thing, this means, that not everyone can read them besides the website owner. This means that if a cookie is released by 'example.com,' it can only be recovered using the same domain. This is done as a way to secure the data and prevent external websites from having access to information which they are not allowed to have.

As a result of the internet's modern architecture, many websites can now release their own cookies. Cookies received from different domains are called third-party cookies. Third-party cookies are usually created by advertising firms as a way for them to collect information about a user as they visit different websites.

Since each website can have its own cookies, many browsers have an option to let users switch their cookies off both for the third-party and the server's domain. Luckily, when you turn off your cookies, you also turn off the third-party cookie for websites.

The exchange of a cookie takes place at the transfer of headers. This happens way before we send the HTML of a web page. The moment the HTML has been sent, it becomes difficult to send a cookie.

Well, learning how to send a cookie is not hard, the most important thing to know is that the HTML exchange should not take place before you have it sent. To define your cookie, you need to write the *setcookie* function. This function comes with the following basic syntax:

Setcookie (name, value, exptre, path, domain, secure, httponly);

If I want to create a cookie with a given name, and only want it to be visible across the web server's domain, this is how it will look:

Setcookie ('visitor', 'Job', time () + 60 *60*24*8, '/');

Accessing cookies

Reading the value of a cookie is not that hard. You can access a cookie by simply using the $_COOKIE array. For example, if you want to check if the current browser has a cookie with the name a visitor stored, we use the code below:

If(isset($_COOKIE['visitor'])) $visitor=$_COOKIE['visitor'];

Remember, you can read a cookie back after you have sent it to the web browser. In other words, if you release a cookie, you won't be able to read it until the browser refreshes the page or another website with access to your cookie happens to return the cookie to your server.

Destroying a cookie

So far you know how to create, access, and read a cookie. When it comes to destroying a cookie, you need to issue it once more and define a date. It is important that all the previous details of your cookie be the same except the timestamp. If they are not identical, you will not succeed in deleting the cookie. So, if you wanted to delete the cookie which we created previously, this is what you need to do:

setcookie('visitor', 'Job', time() - 2592000, '/');

Make sure that the time indicated should be outdated.

HTTP Authentication

The HTTP authentication also makes use of the web server as a means to control passwords and users of the system. This is appropriate for those web applications which require users to sign in.

For the HTTP authentication to be applicable, PHP has to transfer the header request which will then begin a dialog with the web browser. Now, for this feature to work, it must be on.

Username and password storage

MySQL is the popular method of storing data such as usernames and passwords. However, as you know, it is not a good thing to store your passwords in a manner in which anyone can easily access it. One of the ways we can avoid this is by using a method called a 'one-way function.'

This is a very easy function, and what it does is that it changes a string of text into a random string. The nature of these functions makes it very difficult for a hacker to reverse it. With the passing of time, we have come to see that the *md5* algorithm can be hacked, the same goes for the *sha1*. Which is why I recommend that you use the PHP hash function. To see how it works, we pass it a *ripemd* version algorithm:

$token = hash ('ripemd128', 'mypassword');

The end result of the token is a random string.

Salting

However, using hash on its own does not provide enough security for the database password because the chances are that if a hacker uses brute force, he will successfully retrieve the password. So, to solve this problem, we use a method called 'salting' before we finally apply the hashing. Salting is a process where we now add our own text to each parameter so that it can be encrypted. This is how it happens:

*$token =hash ('ripemd128', '**mysaltstring**mypassword');*

In the above example, the *mysaltstring* has been attached to the password.

Using sessions

You have already used this in the practical example. Sessions help you monitor what your visitors are doing when they move from one page to another.

Starting a session

To start any session, you must write or put the *session_start* function before the HTML, in the same way, that cookies are set. Now, if you want to save the session variables, you need to allocate them to the $_SESSION array by doing this:

$_SESSSION ['variable'] = $value;

If you want to read your session, you can do this:

$vartable =$_SESSION['vartable'];

Ending a session

The function *session_destroy*, will help you end or destroy a session.

Conclusion

Having read every chapter in this book, now you know how to write PHP code that can connect to the database, you understand the different database concepts, you can build a complete user registration system, and many more. Well, we also believe that you know how to write an innovative PHP code. Remember, PHP is an easy to understand language, and if you can give yourself sufficient time to practice, you will become a professional in PHP.

If you can master the basic fundamentals explained in this book, then you will be ready to start building PHP applications. PHP is an incredibly useful programming language which can help you develop robust applications. To become a great PHP developer, you have to put in a lot of effort. An excellent programmer should stay updated with the latest changes in the world of PHP to learn and understand the vital things that everyone has to know. Most importantly, I will suggest that once you have finished reading this book, the next step is to look for PHP books that have practical tests you can try. Get in-depth PHP books to help you understand the concepts better.

In this book, we have set the path for you continue exploring and learning deeper PHP concepts.

The next step you should take is writing your own PHP code. Practice every day until you master it.

Thank you and good luck!